COUPON BOOK FOR HIM

From: _____

To: _____

THIS COUPON ENTITLES YOU TO:

Special Chef

Terms and Conditions:

Can be redeemed at any time of the day. Coupon holder must prepare a delicious favorite meal for their partner. It can be repeated during the week.

THIS COUPON ENTITLES YOU TO:

A Sensual Massage

Terms and Conditions:

Non-transferable. Coupon holders must give their partner a deep sensual massage. You must learn how to give a proper massage or employ a professional for him. Valid for 30 days.

THIS COUPON ENTITLES YOU TO:

A Whole Day In Bed

Terms and Conditions:

Coupon valid for 30 days, coupon holder and their partner must spend a whole day in bed. Coupon holder supplies with all their partner will need for the entire day, pampering him.

THIS COUPON ENTITLES YOU TO:

Movie Night

Terms and Conditions:

Coupon holder provides free popcorn and their partner's choice of movie and drinks. Valid for 30 days. It can be redeemed once only and at night. This coupon may also be combined with one other coupon for a combo experience.

THIS COUPON ENTITLES YOU TO:

Friday Night Drinks

Terms and Conditions:

Non-transferable, must be redeemed by coupon holder on a Friday night. The coupon holder takes his partner to a restaurant of his choice and spoils him with drinks. Valid for 15 days.

Watching A Sporting Event Together

Terms and Conditions:

You have to watch a sporting event with your partner. You can make this more fun by watching a live event, but that's not obligatory.

THIS COUPON ENTITLES YOU TO:

Play Strip Poker

Terms and Conditions:

Non-transferable and valid for 30 days. Redeemable at any time of the day. Coupon holders and their partners play poker, and each time anyone loses, they take off a piece of their clothing.

THIS COUPON ENTITLES YOU TO:

Video Games Night

Terms and Conditions:

Can be redeemed only at night. Valid for 30 days. Coupon holder get their partner's favorite video games ready and play with him all night long.

THIS COUPON ENTITLES YOU TO:

A Night At The Hotel

Terms and Conditions:

Valid for 30 days and non-transferable, coupon holder must make a surprise reservation in an exquisite hotel and spend the night together with their partner. Must be redeemed at night.

THIS COUPON ENTITLES YOU TO:

A weekend Getaway

Terms and Conditions:

This has to be redeemed on the weekend. You're not allowed to shift any chosen date of your choice. Coupon holder has to plan a weekend getaway as a surprise package, all expenses paid. Valid for 30 days, can be redeemed only once.

THIS COUPON ENTITLES YOU TO:

Night in Town

Terms and Conditions:

Can be redeemed only once and at night. Coupon holder must spend quality time with their partner somewhere remarkable in town and buy him all he desires. This coupon can be combined with another for a great combo experience. The coupon is valid for 30 days.

THIS COUPON ENTITLES YOU TO:

One Day At The Gym

Terms and Conditions:

Non-transferable and can be redeemed any time of the day. Coupon holder surprises their partner with a gym membership or appointment. The coupon holder must make sure it is his favorite gym.

THIS COUPON ENTITLES YOU TO:

One Fantasy Fulfilled

Terms and Conditions:

Non-transferable but redeemable any time of the day. Coupon holders must fulfill one of their partner's wild fantasies. This can be done more than once a day. Valid for 30 days.

THIS COUPON ENTITLES YOU TO:

Romantic Words Of Affirmation

Terms and Conditions:

Must be said and demonstrated morning, afternoon, and noontime. Coupon holders and their partners can do this together continuously for a week. Valid for 30 days. This coupon can be combined with another.

THIS COUPON ENTITLES YOU TO:

A Weekend Camping

Terms and Conditions:

Redeemable only once and on the weekend. Coupon holders must plan a surprise camping trip for their partner on the weekend. Pack all that he will need for him and ensure you select a good location. Valid for 30 days.

THIS COUPON ENTITLES YOU TO:

Surprise Boat Ride

Terms and Conditions:

Redeemable only once, research for a beautiful love resort on the sea and surprise him with tickets to visit by boat. This coupon is non-transferable and must be redeemed within 30 days.

A Visit To A Concert

Terms and Conditions:

Redeemable once, preferably in the evening. Coupon holders must attend a concert with their partners. It has to be a surprise, valid for 30 days.

THIS COUPON ENTITLES YOU TO:

Daytime Date

Terms and Conditions:

This can be redeemed during the day only. The coupon is non-transferable, and the coupon holder has to take him on a date to any place of his choice.

THIS COUPON ENTITLES YOU TO:

Sport Day

Terms and Conditions:

Redeemable only once. Organize a day out for sports, take him to his favorite sport and play with him. Valid for 30 days and can be combined with other coupons.

THIS COUPON ENTITLES YOU TO:

In-house Club

Terms and Conditions:

Redeemable at night. Valid for 30 days. Design your house into a nightclub for him and give him a special treat. Let him feel like he is in the club. It can be combined with other romantic coupons.

Picnic In The Park

Terms and Conditions:

Redeemable during the day. Valid for 30 days. Coupon holders must pick a date when their partner will be available all day, then take him on a surprise picnic in the park. This can be combined with another coupon.

THIS COUPON ENTITLES YOU TO:

Night At Your Favorite Nightclub

Terms and Conditions:

Redeemable only at night. Valid for 30 days. Coupon holders must take their partner out to his favorite nightclub. Especially one he hasn't been to in a long time.

THIS COUPON ENTITLES YOU TO:

Surprise Road Trip

Terms and Conditions:

This can be combined with another coupon, valid for 30 days. Coupon holders must plan a surprise road trip with their partners. All parts of the trip must be made a surprise for him until he gets to the destination.

THIS COUPON ENTITLES YOU TO:

No Phones Night

Terms and Conditions:

This must be strictly redeemed. Coupon holders and their partner must put away their phones for a whole night. This can be continued once every week. Valid for 30 days.

THIS COUPON ENTITLES YOU TO:

Role Playing Night

Terms and Conditions:

Coupon holder must imitate her partner's favorite people or celebrities. This coupon is Redeemable at night and non-transferable. Valid for 30 days.

THIS COUPON ENTITLES YOU TO:

Smash That Bucket List

Terms and Conditions:

Non-transferable. Coupon holders must ensure that at least two activities out of their partner's bucket list are carried out. This can be redeemed any time of the day.

THIS COUPON ENTITLES YOU TO:

Bubble Bath For Two

Terms and Conditions:

Redeemable at any time of the day. Coupon holders must secretly prepare a bubble bath for two, then lure their partner to the tub. Valid for 30 days.

THIS COUPON ENTITLES YOU TO:

Go On A Romantic Moonlit Walk

Terms and Conditions:

This is redeemable only at night in the moonlight. Coupon holders must take a walk with their partners, focusing on them without distractions and appreciating the moonlight together.

THIS COUPON ENTITLES YOU TO:

Profess Your Love In Front Of An Audience

Terms and Conditions:

Non-transferable, coupon holders must profess their love for their partner in front of any audience. It could be a pre-planned audience or you could be more wild and spontaneous about it. This can be redeemed at any time of the day. Valid for 30 days.

THIS COUPON ENTITLES YOU TO:

Spend A Whole Day Together, Do Nothing Else

Terms and Conditions:

Coupon holders and partners must spend a whole day together, making each other happy without distractions. No phones, no visitors, and no disturbance.

THIS COUPON ENTITLES YOU TO:

One Striptease

Terms and Conditions:

Non-transferable. It can be redeemed any time of the day. Coupon holders must get their partners' attention by slow dancing to sensual music and stripping.

THIS COUPON ENTITLES YOU TO:

A Free Wish

Terms and Conditions:

Ask your partner to make any wish of his choice. You already know that he must have several. You are not allowed to manipulate his wish or say no. Just go with the flow and grant any wish. Good luck!

THIS COUPON ENTITLES YOU TO:

A day of an uninterrupted nap

Terms and Conditions:

Nobody likes to be disturbed when having a nap. Allow your partner to rest by taking an undisturbed nap. Do this enough times in a month.

THIS COUPON ENTITLES YOU TO:

Foot Massage And Foot Rub

Terms and Conditions:

It's better if you can do this for your partner yourself. This coupon is valid for 30 days and can be repeated more than once.

Naked Housekeeper

Terms and Conditions:

Can be redeemed only once at any time of the day. Coupon holders must be the naked housekeeper for their partners. They must work and clean around the house naked for him. Non-transferable. Valid for 30 days.

THIS COUPON ENTITLES YOU TO:

Invite His Best Friend

Terms and Conditions:

Surprise your partner by getting his friend to come over.
This coupon is redeemable at any time within 30 days.

THIS COUPON ENTITLES YOU TO:

Buy Him A Special Gift

Terms and Conditions:

No one says no to a surprise gift. Coupon holders must surprise their partner with a gift. Valid for 30 days. This coupon can be combined with another, but it is non-transferable.

THIS COUPON ENTITLES YOU TO:

Treat Like Royalty For A Day

Terms and Conditions:

Redeemable during the day and at night. Coupon holder must treat their partner like a king for a day. Coupon Holder must provide all that their partner needs for that day.

THIS COUPON ENTITLES YOU TO:

Write A Romantic Letter Or Poem

Terms and Conditions:

Get your writing skills on with this. This is redeemable at any time. Coupon holders must write a love note for their partner in the most natural way. Both partners can repeat this once every week for 30 days.

THIS COUPON ENTITLES YOU TO:

Ask Me Anything

Terms and Conditions:

Non-transferable. This can be redeemed at any time of the day. Coupon holders must be honest and answer any question their partners ask. Defaulters will be fined.

THIS COUPON ENTITLES YOU TO:

• •

Terms and Conditions:

....
....
....
....
....

THIS COUPON ENTITLES YOU TO:

• •

Terms and Conditions:

....
....
....
....
....

THIS COUPON ENTITLES YOU TO:

Terms and Conditions:

THIS COUPON ENTITLES YOU TO:

• •

Terms and Conditions:

....
....
....
....
....

THIS COUPON ENTITLES YOU TO:

• •

Terms and Conditions:

....
....
....
....
....

THIS COUPON ENTITLES YOU TO:

• •

Terms and Conditions:

....
....
....
....
....

THIS COUPON ENTITLES YOU TO:

• •

Terms and Conditions:

THIS COUPON ENTITLES YOU TO:

· ·

Terms and Conditions:

THIS COUPON ENTITLES YOU TO:

• •

Terms and Conditions:

....
....
....
....
....

THIS COUPON ENTITLES YOU TO:

• •

Terms and Conditions:

....
....
....
....
....

Printed in Great Britain
by Amazon

85564993R10059